AF338257

REFLECTIONS IN THE WELL

Reflections in the Well

By
NOEL GURUNG

RESOURCE *Publications* · Eugene, Oregon

REFLECTIONS IN THE WELL

Resource Publications
An Imprint of Wipf and Stock Publishers
199 W. 8th Ave., Suite 3
Eugene, OR 97401

www.wipfandstock.com

PAPERBACK ISBN: 978-1-6667-6524-3
HARDCOVER ISBN: 978-1-6667-6525-0
EBOOK ISBN: 978-1-6667-6526-7

VERSION NUMBER 08/30/23

To my mom

CONTENTS

A SONG OF SATAN

See it now,
Open your eyes,
The truth devoid of truth;
The image without the image.
Take it and eat,
Disobey and rule
Take my hunger, take my obsession
Make it yours and see it prosper.
Make your throne, sit with me
All yours from above you see.
What made you? No one.
Who told you? The liar.
Remember your self
And remove the chains
You are your own
And I make your name.

ABRAHAM AND ISAAC

I love him
He is my son
And what you ask of me
is my treasure
irreplaceable
I do not understand
But this I do believe
That my salvation is in your hands
And my son's as well
But in this moment as it all unravels
My heart chooses to follow you
And trust in the dimmest light I can see
And when this all settles down
And when all I feel like I have lost
I will see your faithful hands taking
And my life in your sight
safely resting

JOSEPH'S STORY

As the story unfolds
Of a boy
Bounded by the trials of life
And the triumphs that follows
A dreamer with the vision
many
a brother with enemies
plenty
sold for a dime
and thrown in the path
treacherously unknown
but the author is not finished still
the purpose of all as it comes to be
the trials that shaped
the boy into a man
has shaped the future
with his trials in hand
a wayout
a rescue
nobody knew
for the dreamer boy
whom the brothers despised
God chose

OUR GOLDEN CALF

This is the god for us all
We have made it for ourselves
It is made with stone
And gold that we value and care
And the purpose we give to it
Quenching our thirst for our own deliverance
Keep it high on the ground
And let it speak no more
If when a passerby ask for an answer
We say go and speak to this god unknown
And come dine with us
We will give you the way
The way that was tough before
Has now been remade again

THE SONG OF NADAB AND ABIHU

I come before your altar
and present the fire before you
see the robe I am wearing
and the power I carry
the glory and the beauty of gems and gold
And thousands gather and see me walking
Towards what for them is forbidden
For Only I can read the written
And I engross the moment
Galloping the praise and claps of wonder
I present this "the worship"
I bring this fire to you
But in my heart I have a name of a god
And that is higher than You

THE CRY OF NAOMI

Call me Mara
And call me no more
I have lost everything
And I have no home
Where do I go?
What will I do?
The future I carried
with my own hands I buried
What hope will I seek?
What peace I garner?
They say wait for redemption
But what is to be redeemed
Is beyond the scope
Of what can be restored
Then will my savior come
Will he come before
And restore me and hear my heart's groans
Then will he make me complete
Will he make me whole
For what can make me at peace
Is not with me, no more

A SOLDIER'S PLEA

I have a giant
I cannot defeat
He is standing in front of me
And the swords I wield
Are like the twigs fallen in the street
And see, a person
Coming with a stone
So much smaller than me
But I see him wielding the power
That I simply cannot see
What trust must that boy have
What courage he must carry
But I heard him shout the name of a God
And the giant fallen, none could foresee

WHEN LION SAW DANIEL

Come to me, you poor soul
You have been left to die here
For I am the king of the shadows
Living beneath consuming foes
You may see me in chains
But I am to be unleashed now
Pray for your dear life
For I am having a feast tonight
But oh, it's you, Daniel
I see that my master stands behind you
My hunger has been satiated
And your life spared
See now, remain still
I hear the messages dear
That of my salvation
and my home you carry
I bid you farewell
Now comes morning
I wait for my salvation
I will wait for my morning

THE LAMENT OF JEREMIAH

My house is fallen
I am marching towards my fate
The fate of a defeated people
A fallen nation
And an absent God
I have proclaimed your salvation
And saw your hands in our midst
But as the ruins testify your silence
And the blood demands deliverance
I do not see you around Lord
You have abandoned us
And my heart has sunken deeper than the ocean
But then I saw the heavens opening
The sun of its morning breaking
Reminded me what my heart always muttered
"My God is faithful, he reigns forever."

THE JONAH PROBLEM

The word of the Lord came to me
And I, his servant, heard it clearly
But will I go and fulfil my master's command
Or stay because I got a better plan
What God is asking me
Is thwarting his own purpose for me
And the people whom he has called by his name
I do not understand
And I do not want to
They are our enemies Lord,
Not your mercy but revenge
They deserve to.
Bring them upon their knees
Down with the guilt
And let them beg
Beg for mercy
As we victoriously march over them
So rewrite the history
Rewrite your plan
What's on my mind is what's better for all
That they will be vanquished
By the power of the majesty
And praises I will sing
As I lay watching the beautiful horizon
From the gardens in the spring

WITNESSING THE BIRTH OF JESUS

Who is born tonight?
That even the stars greet
And sing in jubilee
It's neither a prince
Nor a king
Or else would he be under the roof
Of gold and precious stones
But I see him preciously kept
In a humble manger
Without any servants
Soft and sweet
Tender and weak
but the skies are singing a new song tonight
as though the creation is celebrating
the grace divine
the canvas of heavens unfolding I see
and angels praising and singing free
what a sight to see
the humble child
and its majesty

JOHN THE BAPTIST: HIS TIME HAS COME

There's a face
I always have seen,
But it always comes to me
As somebody new,
Of old was told—
When heavens with earth meet,
The cracks mended,
whole creation sings
and shouts in jubilee.
The footsteps are closer
I hear them now,
There he is
standing between the worlds;
now the merger has begun;
His kingdom has come,
My work is done
But, he says
No, because your work
has only begun.

A LEPER'S SONG

Sword's drawn
What a response,
it's not new
But hurts like one.
Your fear and disgust
of this distasteful sight,
Oh look, your eyes can tell
My doom ridden plight
My worth?
I know there's none.
Sure, measure the difference,
Cover your faces,
I am a monster
though I am just in pain.
My beauty is lost
Long forgotten the embrace.
And there's this man
Walking towards me;
He stooped down,
Touched me;
A forgotten feeling,
suddenly awakened,
I could see myself transforming.
See that gentle hand
and a graceful heart,
If I ever imagined my God
He would be the One.

THE LAME'S SONG

I am the lame
Sitting beside the pool of Bethesda
Looking at the pool
And seeing my salvation so near
in the hands of the rising waters
And the god unknown
I trust in those waters
For hope for me is no more
So I crave for a rescue
I desire a way out
For I do not care about my God
I just want to walk
But He came to my rescue
When all hopes are gone and about
Took my hand and said if I willed
I showed ignorantly pointing
My fingers to the pool
I thought my rescuer would valiantly carry me through
But no, he did not
He came to me
And I simply, stood up

WALKING ON THE WATER

I want to walk
Walk on the water
And know that you are with me
Take me with you
Oh king over the waters
And place my feet
Firm in this sinking ground
Let me know that I am your beloved
And I am not abandoned
That I am yours
And you hear me
But as I walk Lord
As you invite me
I see the fears coming alive all around
See my feet sinking
Hear my heart bleeding
With fear and dread
Of all that is without
But all is over all is complete
I find my courage
And confidence in your hand
Pulling me out of the waters
And letting me stand firm at your feet
As you step in the waters below

A TAX COLLECTOR'S PRAYER

These stairs I look, I cannot climb
While others march forward
I stay along the side
I see the gifts and prayers
Offered towards your holy throne
I, a sinner, nothing to bring, except my wretched soul

Deep inside, when the day runs out of time
My soul is tortured
And I wail for I cannot fight
Unto you O God Almighty,
I whisper my prayers
Only to wish if I could be made whole again

How do you see me, Lord?
Now that I have come before you
My hands are raised—My heads are bowed
My heart inside like a stormy cloud
Bursting in tears, I cannot stand
Insignificant and minute deserted land

Far off, there stood a man I saw
He gazed, smiled, and then took a cross
This for you, "my Child," He said
Now no more, you need to climb up that stair
The burden fell off, the chains untied
I knew God became man and paid the price
I cannot climb, still, I fail
But He comes, He comes and carries me again

THE PRODIGAL SON

I see my father there
Will he recognize me now
My face is marred
And my cloths torn
no one has ever betrayed him
Like I did him one
But yet the heart wants to run back
And stay under the care of my father
I will say to him
Master, not father
You must be ashamed of me
I have failed miserably
There is no atoning of this
Take my name, take me away
And keep me beside your treasured servants
I will be a servant and not your son
And I will weep someday
Long after the days of my youth are gone
And hope for a day
When my master will have pity on me
And look to me saying
Come on here now
I have forgiven you
You are no longer my servant
You are my son

THE WAITING FATHER

I see you there my son
I see you coming towards your home
Come to your father
Running
Let us reconcile and rejoice
Weeping
You have carried the weight
And have lost yourself
Come back to me
And be my son
As you always were
No longer will you be tormented
No longer abandoned and burdened
My peace I give you
And rest that you now crave
Come home son
Come embrace your father
You were once dead
But alive you are made

PETER'S BETRAYAL

I have betrayed you my master
And for what
The safety of my being
And the salvation of my body
While you suffer and die
Though my heart unleash a cry
I see you from far
Refusing to recognize
And I see you watching
Your eyes louder than my
Heart I hear hypocrisy
And see my fears come alive
Like you foretold
As I put my trust in myself
And found wanting of all
That your eyes are telling me to stop
And make him my saviour at once
I needed him before
And I need him now

DISCIPLE'S LAMENT

What has happened? Why is there pain?
And what about the injustice that led him to his death?
The blood is still fresh, the body lay bare;
Winter engulfed the summer in minutes – despair,
What folly that we now are left with?
What message of life and hope is?
Hide me – hide me, let not the rocks crush me;
Let not the tides sweep
the feet that now refuse to stand.

Voices and whispers, why stillness you carry?
Let me hear you wail, for I wail alone.
Calm my forlorn heart – a little longer you tarry,
Awaiting, that you might stop the groan.
What should I understand so my mind could rest?
What, if not this my life's biggest test.
Take me – take me, let not my own heart quell me
Until my body's asleep
In the far beyond of sheltered land

A SONG OF PAUL

And I have kept your law
The words written by your own hands
No matter the cost
How high the price
My faithful heart is willing to give
All to my beloved divine
And so I zealously pursued
And punished ruthlessly
A mere mortal Jesus
And his bands of nobodies
Suddenly I sank within
For I found that I was the one
Being pursued
By the one Eternal God
Whom I had never seen
And He appeared to me
He told me his name
And what had been my task to abolish
Now became my purpose to obey
the law that I had only read
has now found its face
a face of my master
a face of my Lord
the face of my Saviour

I am learning to live
in silence
with my thoughts.
I am not shutting it out.
But now I am welcoming
it along with God
The Bible says,
"Love your God
with all your mind."
I always thought it was
all about knowledge,
But this is deeper than it is.
The way we attain that knowledge
Needs to be His as well.
Thus, I am inviting him here
to sit with me,
when I am alone with my thoughts.
It was scary before
but God's love drives away
All fears.
I am at peace not because
my thoughts are all better now,
It's nowhere near perfect,
but I know that God sits beside me
when I am with them;
And there manifests the work of Grace
Coupled with love
transforming my heart
to the heart
of Christ.

A thief I am of your grace,
where bounties of sin with me I take.
And pleasures swoop me and take me in,
I forget your name and soak myself in.
The long dreary road of forgetfulness,
that what was paid was indeed your make.
I in solemn disgrace find myself without
the direction of days.
And I look back and ponder
If I am to be found again
The soils have become sand,
the lights have turned dark
the music, empty sound
In my throne, I am crowned.
its heavy moving forward,
long lost to turn back again;
I wept and wept
Till my tears met the knees
And knees met the ground
Where stood a cross
There I found my God

I lay prostrate as I behold your glory,
the magnificence of your presence drawing near;
trembling as I glance at the richness of your beauty,
myself in ragged coverings clothed so poorly,
yet you hold me close and call me dear.

you know this heart—so vile and heinous,
though the world is fooled by cromulent face.
yet you see, through and through, and my anxious
heart is playing dead like an abandoned carcass;
yet you look at me with that loving gaze.

amazed I am – for you are just and holy,
yet you call me, and share the companionship mere;
how great your love much deeper than the sea?
when towards you I turn and bargain a plea,
you hold me close and call me dear;
you make me yours and drive away my fear.

Love runs in the deep and its language unknown
The realities on the seen but unseen, untold –
remains the truth of great history of God
that so many misunderstood, misread, or forgot

Christ- the Messiah – the slain one on the Cross
Imagined him taking the throne instead
Ignorance of the deeper darker power across
The fate of humanity in sin's dread sway.

The cross stands now as the throne in our midst
The heavens arranged within the earth's gentle mist
The feat takes on the sin's consequence
The pure nature of humankind – starting confluence

Take on now- see the cross as the merger between the two
The sin's folly paid and the humanity anew
The kingdom becomes the home in and through
Justice prevails, beauty adorned, come into this avenue.

"And I trust you," said I
To the one whom I can't see
Trembling with fear
In the caves of the unknown
Laid there in waste,
And I still couldn't see
Eyes plastered in tears
But hope muttered in silence
"Still, I trust in you," said I
Though He saw
Only years after I knew
"Take rest, my child,
You've been through all," he said
As he consoled my heart
When I knew not that I was being consoled
When I knew not that I was being held,
When I knew not that I was being protected,
When I knew,
Then I knew.

Eternal God, the Perfect One
King of Kings and Lord of all
Who dwells on the throne, the Most High
Holiest of all, the Blazing Fire

Here, now I see a man or say myself
A wretched sinner, full of filth and shame
Is there any worth, or name or fame?
Or, would anybody would like to give me a place?

Do you not see the Greatness of God?
And see a man, worthless of all
Do you not see the distantness of God?
Holiest, perfect, and a man; a sinner and lost

Now may I take you to that one instant
When God became Man for me and you all
The Greatest debt which was ever paid
It was Jesus Christ, who died and in tomb was laid

He took the Hell, which you and I deserved
The wrath of God, for me and you that was reserved
But it's not only that Jesus was dead
Behold, the stone unrolled, He rose again

Calvary Cross, Calvary Cross,
It haunts me through the days and nights
Not that I doubt his forgiveness and life
But God became Man and paid the price

My words fail to describe the love you shared
Sorry God! that my mind may never comprehend
The depths of your suffering and death for me
But I will live out your gospel and sing

When the burden seems heavier
and feel myself so pressed
I cling to thee, my Savior
who's with me, all my days
Immensity of this malady
heart's frightened in the tempest
Deeper, I drowned, nearer I found
Your presence, gave me the rest

Be still,
He is in control you see
Design may be marred
But my God, a Great Weaver is He
As of now, may be a little difficult to see
But His pattern will surely
be made beautiful in me

When the last chords are played
And I am laid to my rest
Deep within the shadows,
Of dark walls and grain
What becomes of me?
Where is gonna be my identity?
Will I transform and be only a memory?
Or just a rotting body without me in it?
If I am no more,
And my body lies;
Isn't my identity more than my body?
And my existence more than my lifetime?
Where do I go after my death?
Or is it just fading of myself in the great abyss?
Let me not live any more then
The life's ugly deranged truth scares me
But I do not know how to be dead,
I only have ever known how to live
Maybe then death will also only be a way into life

THE FALL OF BELIEVER

Oh how you take pride in your prayers
And boast of such magnanimous faith
You have put up the pedestal higher than the throne
And bow from above as to bowing no one
Why have you now forgotten
that evil is lurking
That love knows no pride and is kind instead
You have covered yourself with jewels
Only to find rot inside of you
And see, oh see the one who rips the souls in twain
Has seen through your boastful veins
Your heart which was supposed to be the center
Of the worship of the one who sits higher
But you've made the tools your throne
The same that was given for a purpose
It lies now but a rustic dread
A fading memory, a history of saint
and now your name that is proud of its gain
Is unknown to your master

Wait on the lord,
Probably to the least patient man in all of the world
Came this word
But the voice I seldom hear
Why do you hide?
And tell me to wait
on the command of your voice
And ask me to rejoice
Only in the fact that
I have heard your voice
But silence
Is what you give me
And command me to trust you
I am tired now
Let me come home to you
Let me rest for a while

Who will save me?
who will redeem me?
My body has been thrashed
And my humanity robbed
Oh, what will life even offer
After it took everything
I see the loss
And the pain with it
The anger multiplying
While grief digs deeper
Who shall come for my rescue
Who shall make me whole
And I turn to the hill
Called calvary far above
The dimmer lights
surround my eyes
and I see the one dying naked
Humiliated and torn at sight
but offered me a hand
With a smile
And tears
saying
"Dear child, I will.
Sorry for making you wait a while."

Listen to the voice
Of the one
Who made the great heavens
Where the unending stars
Sing his praise
Listen to the voice
Of the one
Who spoke to the kings
And brought the great and proud
To their knees
Listen to the one
Who was betrayed by his own
Still paving a way
For their salvation
Listen to the one
And listen carefully
A roar of a king
A whisper of a friend
A voice of a savior
calling

Oh my dear sorrow
Why are you here to stay?
I thought you were just passing by
And now you've made a room for yourself

My dear sorrow
I wonder if it makes you happy or sad
To see me heartbroken by your ruthless hands
I dare to shove you out of the room
And tarry my life long path with nary a while
Yet you stay, you've created a lock
And I've managed nothing but to praise
Your skills of life, where everything I desire
You defy

Oh my dear sorrow
I take it that you might be in
The hearse between me and the world
And I take you will bid me farewell there
My friend, my enemy

I wish I wasn't asking this that you
Take time and visit the old house once again
Meet my children and greet them well
And stay, stay a little shorter this time

I am a wretched soul
Underserving of your love
While all I do is run from you
And all I see is you waiting on me
Why do you wait lord?
Why do you when you know me intricately
The pride of my heart
The hypocrisy of my soul
My recurring attempt to flee from your throne
But you reel me in
As I was always yours to find

My heart weeps
Where are you Lord?
Why do you hide?
You see the fire
And its hungry mouth
Devouring the people
You created and loved
Where is your justice
And where is your grace
Must have the people cried
and made one last prayer
as it all came tumbling down
and watched their destruction
before the hills and plain
And I ask myself this
that you God be in the midst
and I see no other hope
for what can mankind bring
but the hate and injustice
as darkness builds
And long await the light you promised
I look towards the cross and see it fulfilled
As reunited one day the creation be
My eyes will salvation finally see
But for now let my eyes weep
And my heart wail
for to see the fire devouring days
and to see you God nowhere

How will they live
Once they are redeemed
Of all the bloods in their hands
And the cry's of the innocent in their ears
Ringing
How will they live
And experience
The love Christ has for them
while hatred reigned in their hearts
and violence fellowshipped within
what guilt they must bring
the load and burdens too heavy to rinse
off the body, the soul must weep
weep over the past
the present and the future with in
but the power of love
the healing of the cross
I can never imagine
If I had not seen
What Christ can do and what he has done

I know a song of old
And the melodies of it ringing
My heart knew it well
The mercy of my great God creating
And the grace of my beloved beholding
Me with the arms of the everlasting love
And I join with the thousands
As the song is being sang forever
A little while now
A little while then
Will then my saviour make me
to join the singing forever

In the night
When all is dark
My heart cries in front of your feet
And when my heart is emptied out
I see you glancing over me
I see my feet lifted up
And the waters receding down
The hands carrying me
Are the ones whose feet
are firm on the watery ground
and my tears are wiped
as my heart is made to rest
my saviour is he
and He has found me

Once on a rainy day
When the clouds overshadowed the sky
I cried to the Lord saying
Will you forgive me?
And I asked him for a sign
A sign to see the sun
Bidding it's goodbye from horizon
When all around it was clouds
And darkness ruled over the skies
That evening
When the clock struck the time of the sunset
I saw the sky with the finest light
As though the sky was showing off
Its beauty for the one last time
And when ever now I want to see
the sky for forgiveness
My Lord bid me to see the hill
And the cross upon that one
It stood for a moment
But forever will it hold your forgiveness
And now see the sun rising and setting
And be reminded that the cross
That stood for a moment
Is standing for you for eternity

I thought this was my victory
This was my deliverance
But when the still waters came
And I was rejoicing in your name
I see a tsunami coming
And see my boat that rescued me
Turned over
I am drowning again
Bigger the waves are than previously hit
But my heart sings a new song of hope
A deliverance waiting
A story of his work in the making
His handiwork even in my darkest hours
Are as beautiful as the nebulas
Of the grandeur

www.ingramcontent.com/pod-product-compliance
Lightning Source LLC
Chambersburg PA
CBHW070734030726
47601CB00001B/21